The
Orient Express

Rob Waring, *Series Editor*

HEINLE
CENGAGE Learnin

Australia • Brazil • Japan • Korea • Mexico • Singapore • Spain • United Kingdom • United States

Words to Know

This story is set on the Orient Express, a train that travels through seven countries in Europe to go from Paris, France, over the Alps to Istanbul, Turkey.

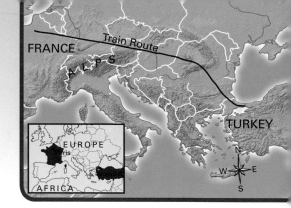

FRANCE
Train Route
ALPS
TURKEY
EUROPE
Paris
AFRICA
N
W E
S

A **The Orient Express.** Read the paragraph. Then match each word or phrase with the correct definition.

The legendary Orient Express became well known in a bygone era as it carried Europe's wealthy and royal passengers between France and Turkey. With its luxurious décor, the Orient Express evokes images of elegance, romance, and mystery. While the routes may be different now, passengers aboard this luxury train can still be pampered with delicious, first-class cuisine and excellent service as they travel through the varied terrain of Europe.

1. bygone era _____   **a.** the natural features of land; the landscape

2. royal _____   **b.** the art and science of cooking

3. décor _____   **c.** bring out a feeling or thought

4. evoke _____   **d.** the decorative environment of a place

5. romance _____   **e.** spoil; take more care of than is necessary

6. pamper _____   **f.** a period of time in the past

7. cuisine _____   **g.** related to or appropriate for a king or queen

8. terrain _____   **h.** a feeling of excitement, adventure, and happiness

The Orient Express

Working on a Legend. Read the definitions of the types of jobs found on the Orient Express. Then label the pictures with the correct <u>underlined</u> words.

A <u>bartender</u> serves drinks at a bar.
A <u>cabin steward</u> cleans and tidies the cabins on the train.
The <u>chef</u> is a skilled cook, especially the main cook in a restaurant.
The <u>maitre d'</u> is in charge of a restaurant and its waiters and waitresses.

1. _____

2. _____

3. _____

4. _____

Working on the Orient Express is a tremendous opportunity for many people.

With its famous **boulevards**,[1] historic buildings, and elegant and relaxed atmosphere, Paris is a city that the whole world often associates with romance. Today, though, at one of Paris's grand train stations, people are not looking for love in the **literal sense**,[2] but romance of another kind, from another time. They want to go back to an age when simply getting somewhere was an adventure, a time when Paris was the departure point for the world's most famous train: the Orient Express.

"Good Morning. How are you?" says an American tourist as he approaches a unique ticket desk that sits in front of a long, peculiar train. The train's deep color, classic design, and antique style stand out against its modern-looking surroundings. The tourist is checking in to board the Orient Express, which was once known as 'the Train of Kings and the King of Trains.' In every detail, the Orient Express evokes the elegant images of a golden age: the beautiful décor and **furnishings**,[3] the shiny wood paneling, the fine china and silver that cover the dining tables, and of course, the service. When it began operating at the turn of the 20th century, the train carried members of Europe's royal families and rich business leaders from Paris to Constantinople, or Istanbul as the Turkish city is now called. These days, this luxurious train still makes the journey from Paris across Europe to Istanbul, but it does it just once a year— and it's a journey some wait a lifetime to take.

---

[1] **boulevard:** wide street, usually lined with trees; an avenue
[2] **literal sense:** the original basic meaning of a word
[3] **furnishings:** furniture, window and floor coverings, and other objects for homes and offices

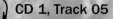 CD 1, Track 05

Skim for Gist

Read through the entire book quickly to answer the questions.

1. What is the reader basically about?
2. About which two groups of people related to the Orient Express does the reader give information?

As the train commences its travels in Paris, passengers settle in for a six-day journey through seven countries across the continent of Europe. It may be a long physical journey, but it's more than that—it's also a voyage into the passengers' own imaginations. Eli, a passenger on this trip, explains that for him it's all about a journey into the past, into history. "What I really wanted to get out of the Orient Express was the feeling of going into—[or] stepping into— a time machine. The idea that I could go back to a bygone era, not just any time, but a time before I was even born, and experience what it would have been like."

For most of the 85 passengers on the run from France to Turkey, the pampering and luxury of this famous voyage are a once-in-a-lifetime treat. Passenger Bill Hummel is typical of many passengers in that he and his wife are celebrating something special. "It has many meanings for us," he says. "My wife had her sixtieth birthday in June and our twenty-fifth wedding anniversary was the twentieth of August."

Passengers come from all parts of the world and many are taking this special trip because they're celebrating a special or private occasion. However, there is one thing that everyone aboard the train seems to have in common: a desire to somehow recapture a lost age and to live an experience that has caught even the **literary**[4] imagination. Karen Prothero, marketing director of the Orient Express explains: "There's a huge fascination for the train, and then of course **Agatha Christie**[5] wrote that famous book, 'Murder on the Orient Express,' which has also helped so much to make it such a famous name."

The Orient Express hasn't continuously operated since the route was first established so long ago, though. In the mid-1940s, after World War II, the possibility of taking an airplane to travel to foreign countries, as well as the rise of the **Iron Curtain**[6] between the East and West, made this type of luxury travel by train impractical. The Orient Express consequently suspended its service until 1997 when it restarted the Paris to Istanbul route.

---

[4] **literary:** related to literature and writing
[5] **Agatha Christie:** (1890–1976) an English crime author, best known for her detective novels
[6] **Iron Curtain:** the political and philosophical barriers or separation between Communist countries and democracies that began after World War II and ended in 1989 with the fall of the Berlin Wall

Identify Cause and Effect

Circle the cause and underline the effect in each of the sentences.

1. The development of airline travel after 1945 meant that luxury train travel was no longer as popular.

2. Some people are attracted to traveling on the Orient Express after reading a famous story about it.

3. The idea of experiencing the past motivates many people to take a journey on the Orient Express.

9

For many people, the attraction of the Paris to Istanbul journey is completely irresistible, and experiencing it is something that they've dreamed about for ages. It's easy to entertain thoughts of taking a long, lazy journey surrounded by magnificent mountain scenery, all while being pampered with service worthy of kings, complete with proper English afternoon tea delivered to one's **travel compartment**.[7]

College professor Robert Franklin explains his motivation for making the trip across Europe. "I've always been a lover of travel," he says, "and always [been] in search of particularly exotic and unusual travel **venues**.[8] The history, the terrain that we are traveling, I mean it's just **soaked with the blood of saints, and warriors, and visionaries**.[9] For me, as a teacher and as a writer, it's really pretty inspiring."

---

[7]**travel compartment:** the small area on a train or ship in which one journeys

[8]**venue:** location; setting or scene

[9]**soaked with the blood of saints, warriors, and visionaries:** influenced by people of historic value: 'saints,' or holy men and women, 'warriors,' or great fighters, and 'visionaries,' or people who planned imaginatively and wisely for the future

As it winds through the magnificent scenery of the Alps, the Orient Express crosses a countryside that consistently displays its finest. Passengers on the train are expected to do no less. As night falls, they begin to prepare for dinner, which on the Orient Express is a formal affair. Passengers must wear their best **attire**,[10] including formal evening suits and dresses. The elegant meals often include fine wines, several courses, and soft music to accompany the dining experience, all adding to the sense that the trip is more than just a train ride. It is a trip where the journey itself is the destination. The idea isn't really to simply arrive somewhere, it's to have an incredible experience along the way—and that includes dining in style. The dinner is always superb,and the atmosphere consistently romantic.

As the evening grows late, the Orient Express rolls along into the night, continuing to make the dreams and wishes of its passengers come true. "It has been a dream for a long time to participate in this little bit of history," says Robert Franklin. "It's hard to imagine a more extraordinary and romantic journey than to travel from Paris to Istanbul on the Orient Express."

---

[10]**attire:** clothing; dress

The next day, while the morning mist hangs around the sleepy fields of Europe, the world's most famous train comes alive. As the Orient Express rolls across eastern Austria, window shades are opened, surfaces are rubbed until they shine, and breakfast is brought to those who choose not to come to the dining car. It all happens quickly, smoothly, and seemingly effortlessly—almost as if by magic.

Making the huge and expensive train operate smoothly isn't magic. Breakfast doesn't appear without staff to prepare it, and a train such as this needs top-class employees. The work on the train has been done by an army of well-trained staff for years. It seems that working on a legend has its rewards. As the team of breakfast waiters rushes to prepare for the morning diners, one can see them smiling as they move through the luxurious furnishings. A cabin steward in charge of making sure that the sleeping cabins are perfectly maintained describes his thoughts about the train. "[It's] a wonderful, wonderful hotel on wheels," he reports.

The staff of the Orient Express knows all about providing first-class service since most of them have also worked in Europe's finest hotels and restaurants. However, when they join the train, they soon find that there are some significant differences between working in a hotel in a city, and working on this 'hotel on wheels.' One bartender talks about the main differences, and how they affect him and his work practices. "Working on a train is very different," he comments, "because you have the scenery which is always changing. In an operational way it's also very different from working in a hotel, so you have to be very well organized." One can imagine the planning that must be involved for a bartender. He must be able to prepare for a trip during which every person expects world-class service but for which there are no alternative resources for supplies, staff, or working conditions.

VICFRES

Primor

There are certainly challenges unique to running a five-star hotel on wheels over a long period of time. These days, the six-day journey through seven countries happens only once every 12 months, but planning for it takes an entire year. Maintaining the proper amount of goods, or stock, on the train is essential. "We move all the time," says the maitre d'. "The train is not like a new train. It wasn't built yesterday, as you know, and then we have limited stock of everything, so we have to try to make it last." The bartender agrees that planning in advance is important, so that they don't run out of food or drinks. "And it's not easy," he explains with a smile. "Instead of a hotel, [where] if you're missing something you just go down to the **canteen**[11] and get it, it's a bit different on the train." These bartenders can't run out for a specific ingredient; they're only able to work with what is available to them on the train—and that's limited by availability, space, and capacity to be preserved.

---

[11]**canteen:** a small store or snack bar

Orient Express has offered a regular seasonal service between Venice and London for over 20 years. Still, the staff seems to learn something new on every journey, and the organization and planning are constantly improving. One of the unusual problems they must continuously face is trying to stay on their feet while creating world class cuisine since the movement of the train can be problematic for the staff. Chef Christian Bodiguel stands in his tiny kitchen and explains just how hard it is for him to work because the train's movement causes everything—including him and his assistant chef—to swing from side to side. "It's very difficult because [as] you can see it's mov[ing] now. For me it's very difficult because we have a small kitchen and it's moving, moving, moving." It's very difficult for the chef and his staff to safely cut and prepare vegetables or cook soups and other liquids in a constantly shifting kitchen.

The situation is no different for the number of bartenders and waiters that must be able to offer food and drinks to their high-class, well-dressed passengers without spilling a drop. While it is challenging, for some the movement of the train actually can help with the work. When asked if working on a train is difficult, one bartender replies, "Ah, it is, but we're used to it, especially working out on the tables." He then goes on to add, "The movement … it keeps you busy. It keeps you very concentrated actually. It's relaxing sometimes."

A chef working on the Orient Express usually faces unusual problems.

The service on the train must consistently meet a high standard of service, and the train's general manager **Claude Gianella**[12] can most likely be credited for that. He explains that for him, service has been the most important aspect of his work on the Orient Express for the past 20 years. "Without being **presumptuous**[13]," he reports, "it has been my main objective for those twenty years to keep the highest possible level of service on what is, after all, a train."

For many in the high-class service industry, the secret of excellent service is to make it all look effortless. To gain this appearance, much of the work on the train is done behind the scenes where the guests can't see the staff hard at work. At various stops along the route, for example, food is loaded onto the train. Several different types of produce come on board at these times, from fresh fruit to freshly caught fish packed in ice. It all has to happen quickly and discreetly so that the food remains under the best possible conditions and the passengers don't see the action. The kitchens are completely restocked within minutes to meet these demands and to keep the train right on track.

---

[12]**Claude Gianella:** [klɔd dʒənɛlə]
[13]**presumptuous:** self-important; showing a lack of respect by doing things not normally permitted

Infer Meaning

1. What does the writer mean by 'behind the scenes'?

2. What does the writer mean by saying they need to 'keep the train on track'?

8P

35028

Traveling through seven countries also involves occasional border challenges as well as some changes that must happen as the Orient Express approaches each border. In each country the Orient Express takes on a new **locomotive**[14] engine and engineer in order to ensure passengers' safety and that the train runs smoothly. But while the locomotive and engineer change, the rest of the staff on each trip stays the same throughout the journey—and often throughout the years, it seems.

The cabin steward who described the train as a "wonderful hotel on wheels" is now in his fourth season with the train, but others have worked on the Orient Express for much longer. "I've been on the Orient Express for thirteen years now," says the maitre d'. Chef Bodiguel has worked even longer: "Fifteen years on board," he says. "Fifteen years I [have] work[ed] here."

---

[14]**locomotive:** a large railroad vehicle with an engine

It's clear that once someone starts working aboard the Orient Express, it's often difficult for them to consider doing anything else. It's obvious that the bartender is very proud of the work he does when he sums up the pleasures of working on the Orient Express: "It's unique. It is. When you go into a train station, the people outside are looking at the train, and you can sort of imagine them thinking how much they'd like to be on that train, and you're on it. I mean you're working on it, which is even better. I mean, it's something very special."

The people who travel and work on the Orient Express have a window-seat view of Europe passing before their eyes and a close up of a bygone era surrounding them. When it comes to romance and adventure while traveling in style, it seems that none of the modern travel options of today can come close to a romantic ride on the Orient Express.

After You Read

1. The main purpose of page 4 is to explain:
    A. what the Orient Express represents
    B. the route of the Orient Express
    C. why the Orient Express departs from Paris
    D. what kind of people ride the Orient Express

2. Which of the following summarizes what Eli says on page 7?
    A. The train ride lets passengers experience another historical era.
    B. The vehicle contains a time machine.
    C. The trip merges contemporary transportation with the past.
    D. The other passengers are trying to flee their realities.

3. According to the story, what helped the Orient Express become so famous?
    A. advertising
    B. a book
    C. the airplane
    D. the Iron Curtain

4. What opinion does the college professor express on page 11?
    A. The trip is only for people with authentic enthusiasm for travel.
    B. The route covers many areas of great historical significance.
    C. Writers and teachers will gain the most insight from the journey.
    D. Knowing about history will enhance the experience of riding the train.

5. The word 'winds' in paragraph 1 on page 12 is closest in meaning to:
    A. rushes
    B. twists
    C. indexes
    D. collapses

6. The cabin steward refers to the Orient Express as _____ luxurious hotel on wheels.
    A. a
    B. the
    C. one
    D. some

7. Which of the following does the writer imply on page 15?
   A. The view in Austria is the most scenic of the ride.
   B. Passengers can request to eat their meals in private.
   C. The staff on the Orient Express are actual magicians.
   D. The waiters are reluctant to prepare breakfast.

8. Which of the following is NOT a difference between working on the Orient Express and at a first-class hotel?
   A. the scenery
   B. planning
   C. organizing
   D. the world-class service

9. When the bartender says "it's not easy" on page 19, he is referring to:
   A. the train
   B. being a bartender
   C. planning in advance
   D. running out of food and drinks

10. Which of these questions cannot be answered with the information on page 20?
   A. What's one challenge faced by the employees on the train?
   B. What kinds of meals does the chef usually prepare?
   C. How does the movement of the train help servers?
   D. What is the Orient Express's regular route?

11. Which word can 'meet' be replaced with in paragraph 1 on page 22?
   A. attain
   B. erode
   C. pose
   D. levy

12. On page 26, which of the following does the writer conclude?
   A. It's tough getting a ticket on the Orient Express.
   B. Most workers on the Orient Express fantasize about being passengers.
   C. Those who get to experience the Orient Express feel privileged.
   D. The people riding on the Orient Express are jealous of the staff.

Travel Temptations

The Orient Express, with its magnificent décor, fine cuisine, and careful attention to details, has long been famous for pampering its guests. Treatment like this was once available only to the rich and famous. Today, however, large hotels, or 'resorts,' worldwide are offering an ever-growing range of luxurious options.

SEA RANCH LODGE, CALIFORNIA

Sea Ranch Lodge is located on the California coast, a two-hour drive north of San Francisco. Its magnificent view of the Pacific Ocean provides an ideal place to relax and enjoy nature. Fine food and wine are two of Sea Ranch Lodge's biggest attractions. The chef is famous in the region and the assistant chef is an experienced specialty baker. In addition, the lodge regularly invites local winemakers to host dinners at the resort where food and wine are perfectly paired and guests can learn more about fine dining. Because it is located far from any large city, Sea Ranch Lodge also offers an unusual option—a dark sky. Guests are encouraged to stay up late to enjoy the beauty of the stars, which are not often visible in the city.

KARMA SAMUI, THAILAND

On the tiny island of Koh Samui off the coast of Thailand lies a resort that provides an astonishing level of luxury. Guests stay in individual houses, or villas, spaced out along the beach. Each one is equipped with a kitchen, dining room, and lounge area, as well as its own medium-sized swimming

Luxury Vacations: Conveniences and Facilities			
Destination	**Specialty**	**Dining Facilities**	**Activities**
Sea Ranch Lodge	magnificent views	fine cuisine paired with fine wine	• learn about wine • enjoy the stars
Karma Samui	extreme luxury	ocean-view dining room or in-room private chef	• learn to cook street food
Canyon Ranch	an introduction to holistic health	healthy food with weight loss guidance	• fitness classes • hiking and biking • cooking lessons

pool. Meals are available in the dining room, or for the height of luxury, guests can have a private chef and waiter prepare and serve their meals in their villa. Karma Samui also offers a 'street food' cooking class in which guests take a guided tour of local markets, buy provisions, and then practice cooking these new specialties when they return to the resort.

CANYON RANCH, ARIZONA

Canyon Ranch calls itself a holistic, or complete, health resort. The owner, Mel Zukeman, says, "For me, our heartfelt intention to help every guest find greater joy in living is what makes us different from all other resorts." The aim is to teach guests how to care for and heal both their bodies and their minds. There are meetings with doctors and alternative healers who offer both conventional and unconventional treatment options. A stay also includes physical activities such as swimming and hiking, dietary guidance, as well as advice on how to reduce stress and better manage personal issues and human interactions in everyday life. Not bad for a week's vacation!

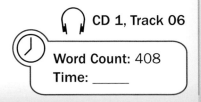

CD 1, Track 06

Word Count: 408
Time: _____

Vocabulary List

attire (12)
bartender (3, 16, 19, 20, 26)
boulevard (4)
bygone era (2, 7, 26)
cabin steward (3, 15, 25)
canteen (19)
chef (3, 20, 21, 25)
cuisine (2, 20)
décor (2, 4)
evoke (2, 4)
furnishing (4, 15)
literal sense (4)
literary (8)
locomotive (25)
maitre d' (3, 19, 25)
pamper (2, 7, 11)
presumptuous (22)
romance (2, 4, 12, 26)
royal (2, 4)
soaked with the blood of saints, warriors, and visionaries (11)
terrain (2, 11)
travel compartment (11)
venue (11)